I0821572

PRIES☥ESS

An illustrated grimoire by
MARCELLA KROLL

INTRO

The hardest part about being an artist is actually just doing the work.I'm not an author, but here I am making a book-formed creationthat feels right. A lot of my life has been like that. I didn't know what I was going to be, but I certainly thought I knew what I would do. Had I not allowed myself to ask for the willingness to be shown how to live I wouldn't be here today. Life has always shown me what it wants me to do. Whether or not I agreed with its choices. The hardest part about accepting what Spirit wants from me is just doing so.

I grew up in a small town, in a small city, in a small state. This is my story in not so many words, but in art, magic, incantations, and experiences. This books is not an instruction manual to get your soulmate, how to make a million dollars, or how to land your dream job. It is instead meant to be a place of refuge, hopefully, a place of comfort, an offering of assistance, and inspiration.

My life experience thus far has been nothing short of painful, exasperating, and sometimes downright cruel. However, in spite of any hardship, I have found it to be quite magical, miraculous, and otherworldly. I truly believe my purpose is to help you find yours, and my hope is that this book helps you navigate your way to it with some helpful tools, words, wisdom, encouragement, and whimsy.

LETTER TO THE READER

Dear One,

When you walk into light everything is visible. The cracks, wrinkles, colors, flaws, sadness, humiliation, joy, regret, excitement, and more are all available for the naked eye to see. To be so deliberate and walk in light is an act of power. As you put yourself on, notice to be vulnerable and fearless, for what you see may not please others or yourself. Yet you are determined to do it anyway. In an act of rebellion I chose to walk in the light. To be visible. To be frightened. To be flawed. To be brave. To get away from everything I was told I would never be free from. To laugh harder at myself then I could be serious. To love myself more than the lie that said I was unloveable.

The purpose of this book is to ignite your own healing and imagination. Do not worry about reading its pages from cover to cover, or getting it right or wrong. Much like bibliomancy (the practice of using books for divination), it's meant to be consumed as needed. In your own magical way, in your own magical time. Let it call to you. Over time you may wish to add your own messages, color, and anecdotes to its pages. I encourage you to make this as personal to you as it is to me. For now, Merry Meet, Merry Part, and Merry Meet Again!

With Love,
Marcella

Dedicated to the Edgewalkers

A Creation Story

My Mother

came from the Sea

My father came from the trees

They went
to the sky
to have
me

was born into the cosmos...

...among the stars I found comfort

And a place
to belong

When it came time to
return to the Earth,

it was much like
a crash landing
of a cosmic
phenomenon

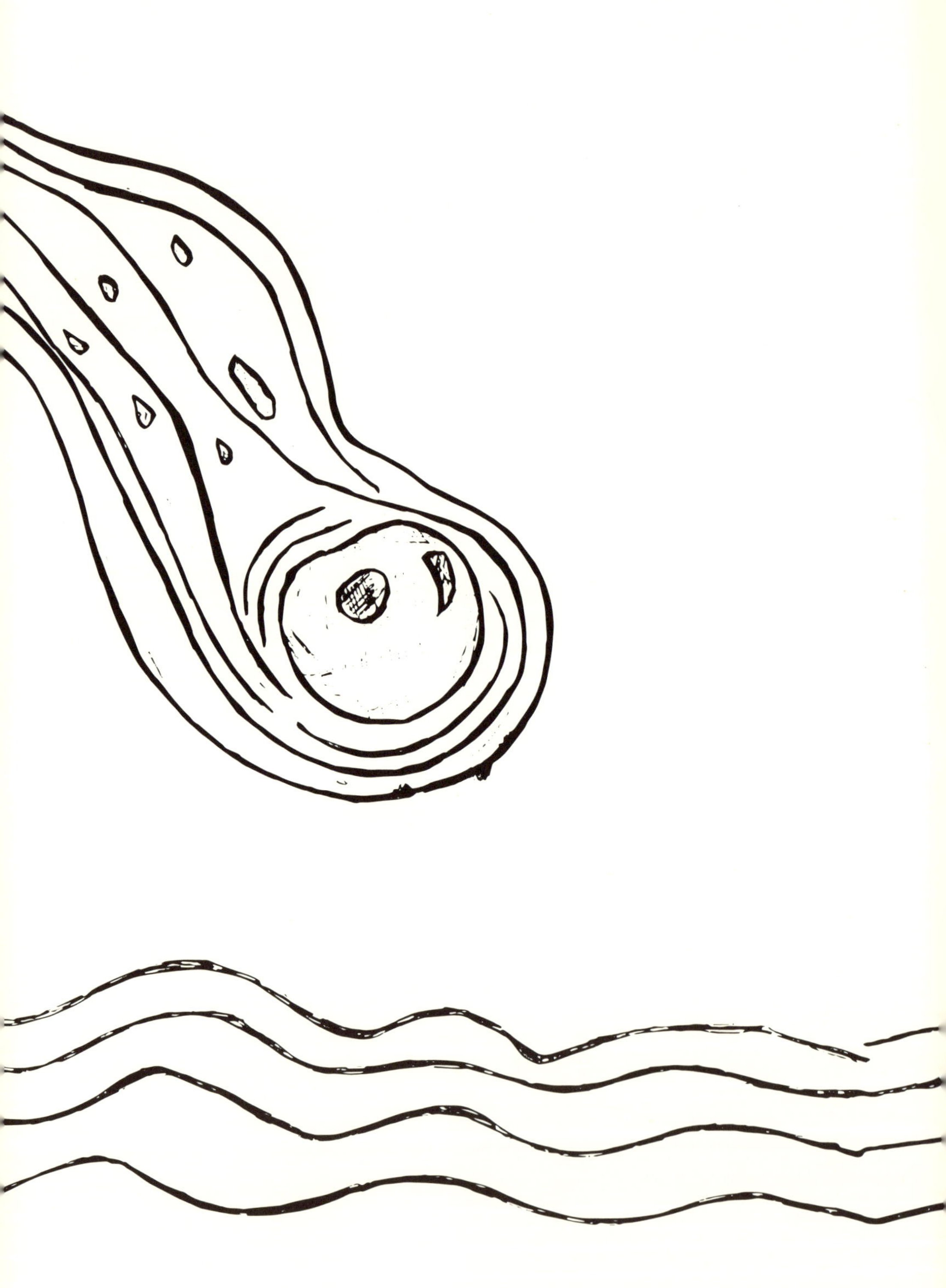

Like a meteorite
I fell to the planet
with a mission,
but quickly forgot all
memories of why I
was to come here.

My whole life has been about remembering.

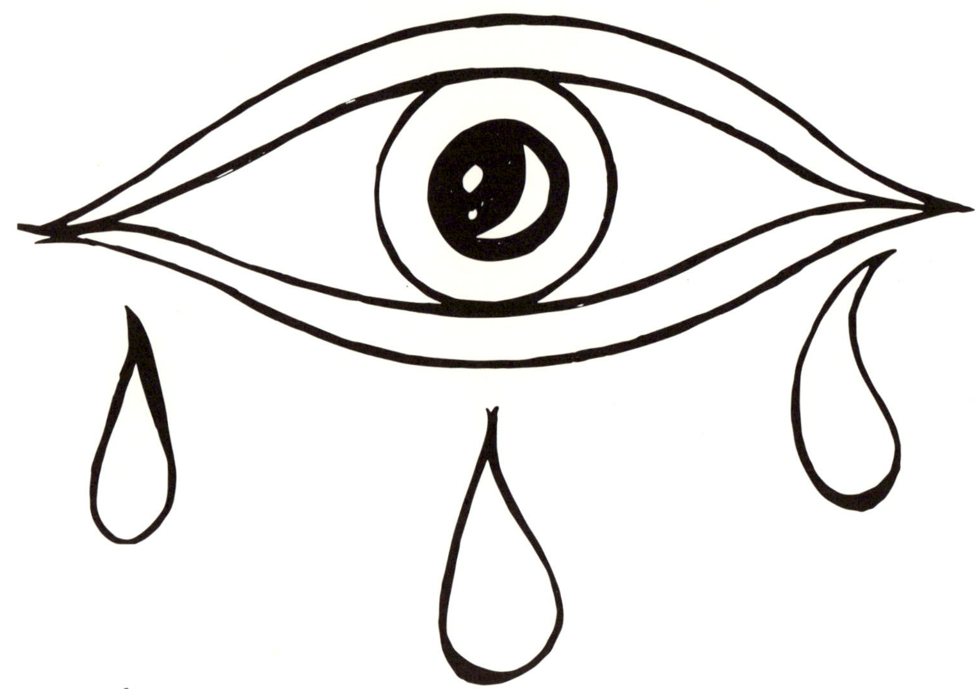

Forgetting what I learned, and remembering what I already know as truth.

The journey through this existance is not for the faint of heart.

For you must stand many wicked trials, illusions, and false ideology.

How this place continues to exist is beyond my understanding

One day humankind will know,
but until then we Star Children
will continue to fall to Earth
and other planets to inhabit,
learn, and participate in one
of the greatist experiments
of all time.

My dream is to one day find a unique and universal understanding of life as it is to be shared.

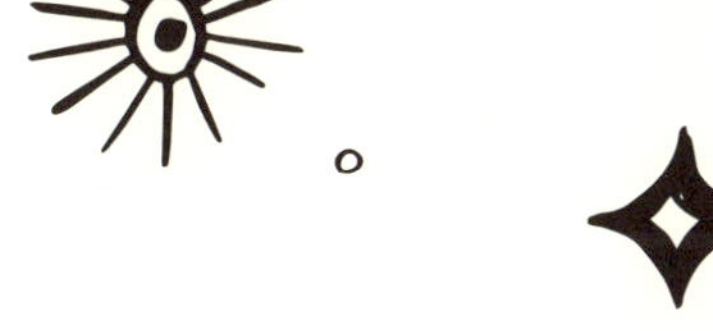

Love conquers all
Fear devours dreams,
and somewhere in
between
we keep moving
and existing

Truth comes in waves
like the ocean

Healing my heart over
time until I find
peace

But for now I stand on
the precipise of a great
awakening

And at the threshold of a
great undoing of all I thought
was fact, but is actually the
greatist fiction of all time.

What I have learned

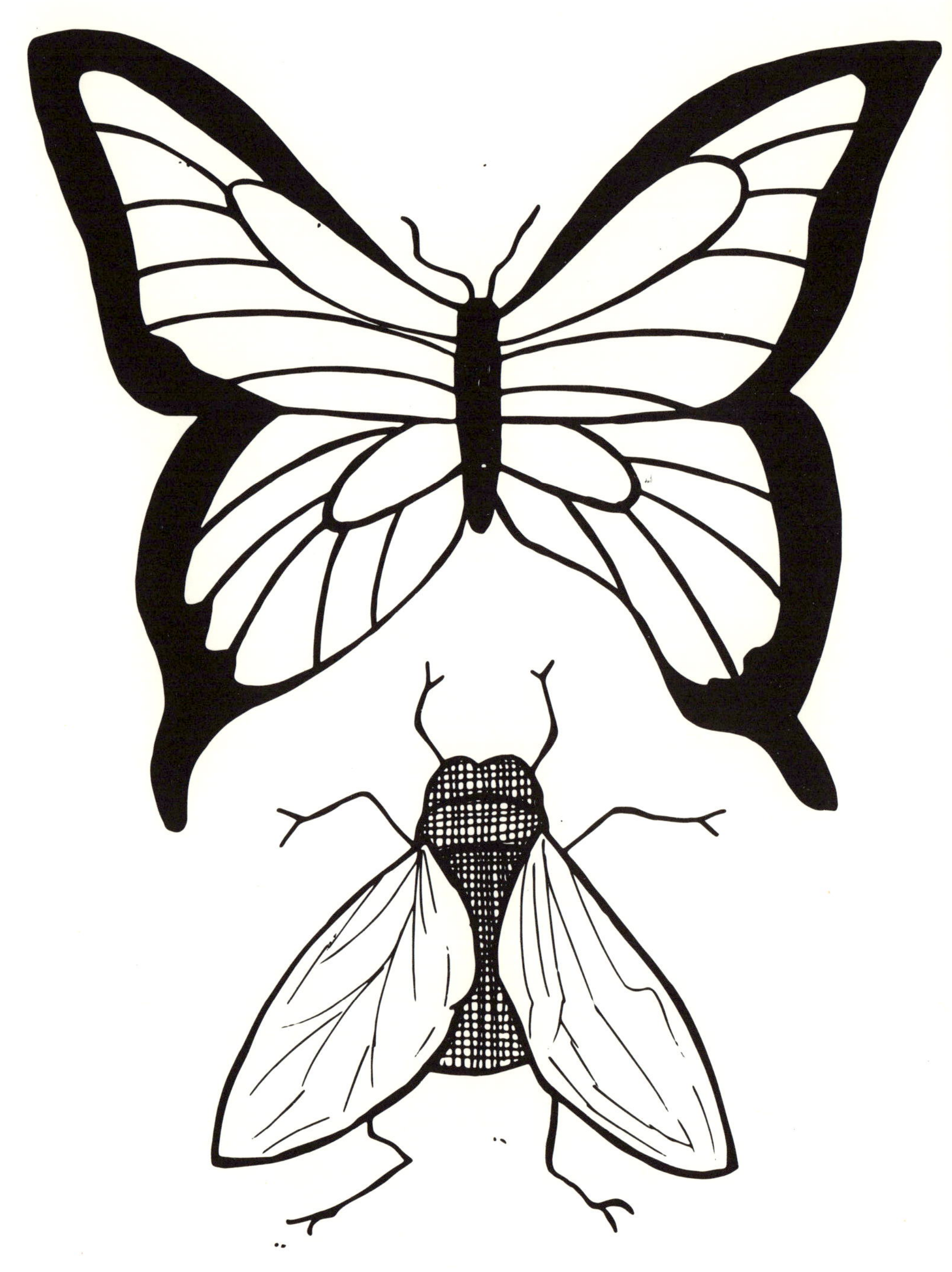

Flies to Butterflies

The greatest prayer
You should send to
your critics is the
gift of evolution

ANCESTOR
HEALING

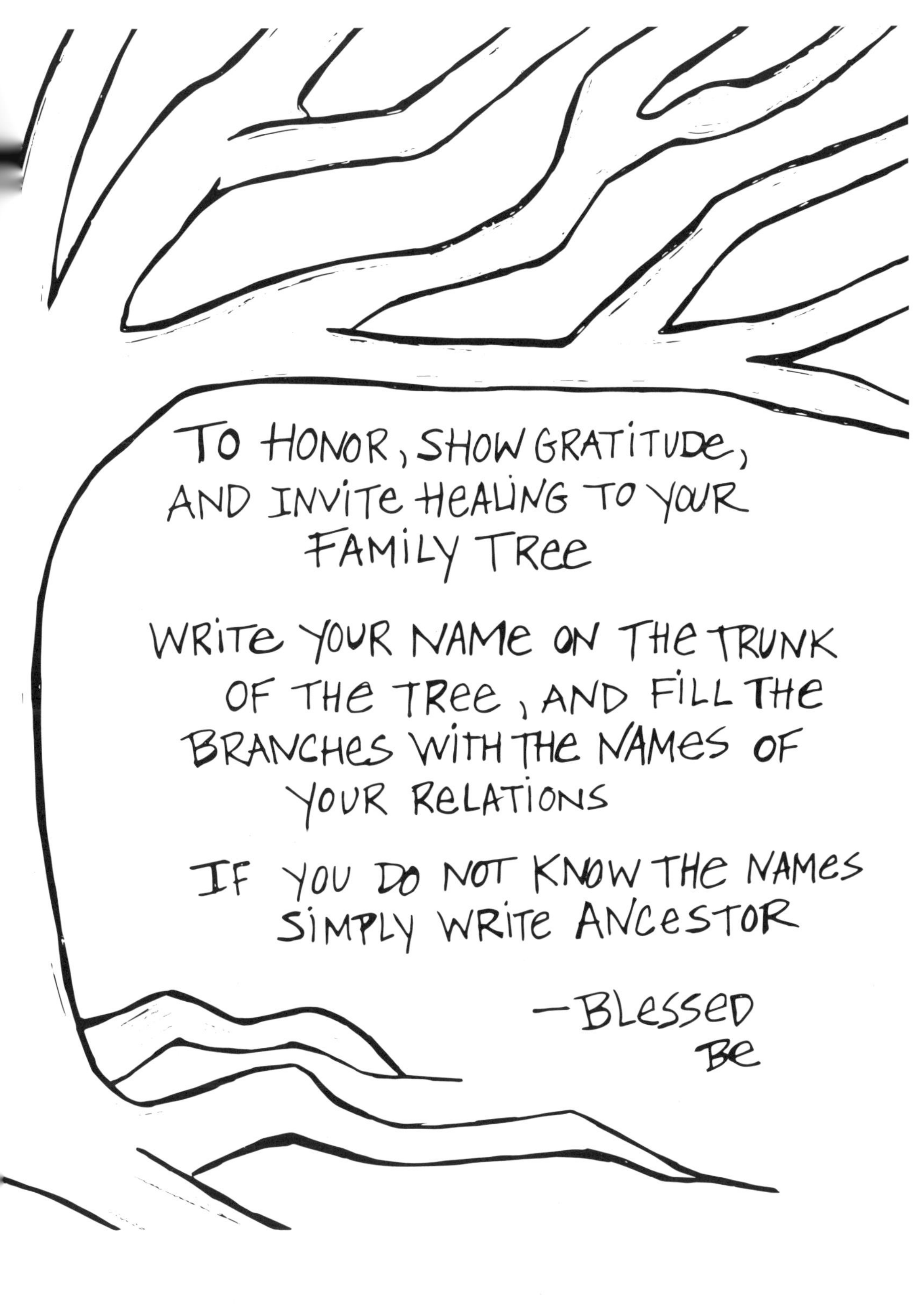
TO HONOR, SHOW GRATITUDE,
AND INVITE HEALING TO YOUR
FAMILY TREE
WRITE YOUR NAME ON THE TRUNK
OF THE TREE, AND FILL THE
BRANCHES WITH THE NAMES OF
YOUR RELATIONS
IF YOU DO NOT KNOW THE NAMES
SIMPLY WRITE ANCESTOR
—BLESSED
BE

3 CARD DRAW

Past

Present

Future

Morning

Noon

Evening

12 CARD YEAR AHEAD READING SPREAD

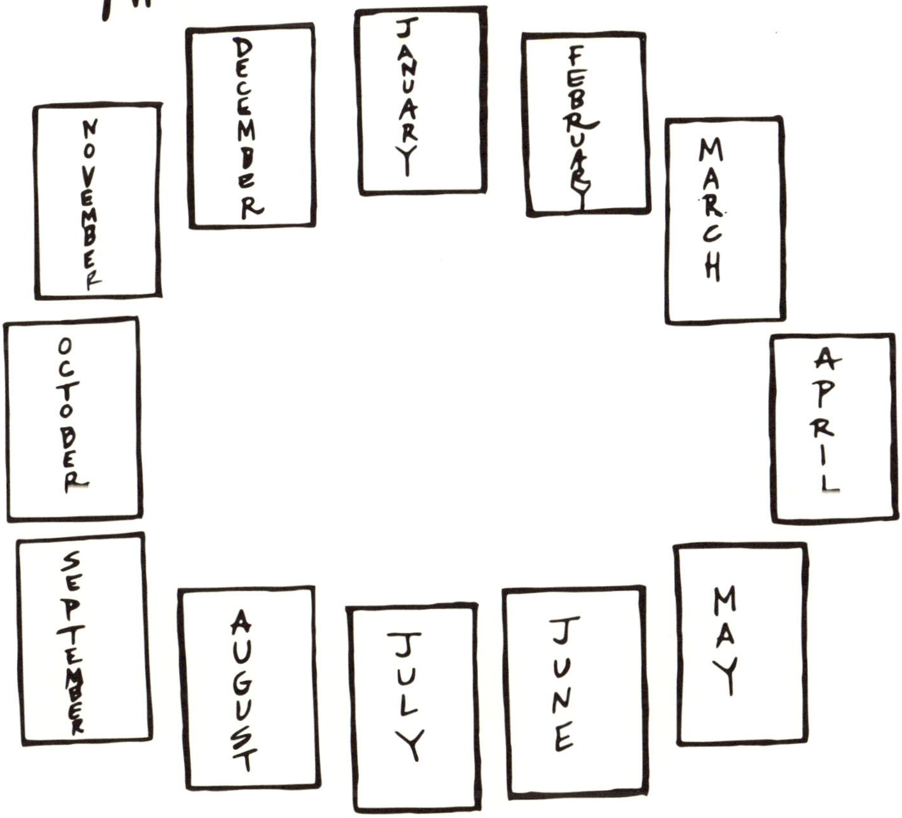

JANUARY

DECEMBER

FEBRUARY

NOVEMBER

MARCH

OCTOBER

APRIL

SEPTEMBER

MAY

AUGUST

JULY

JUNE

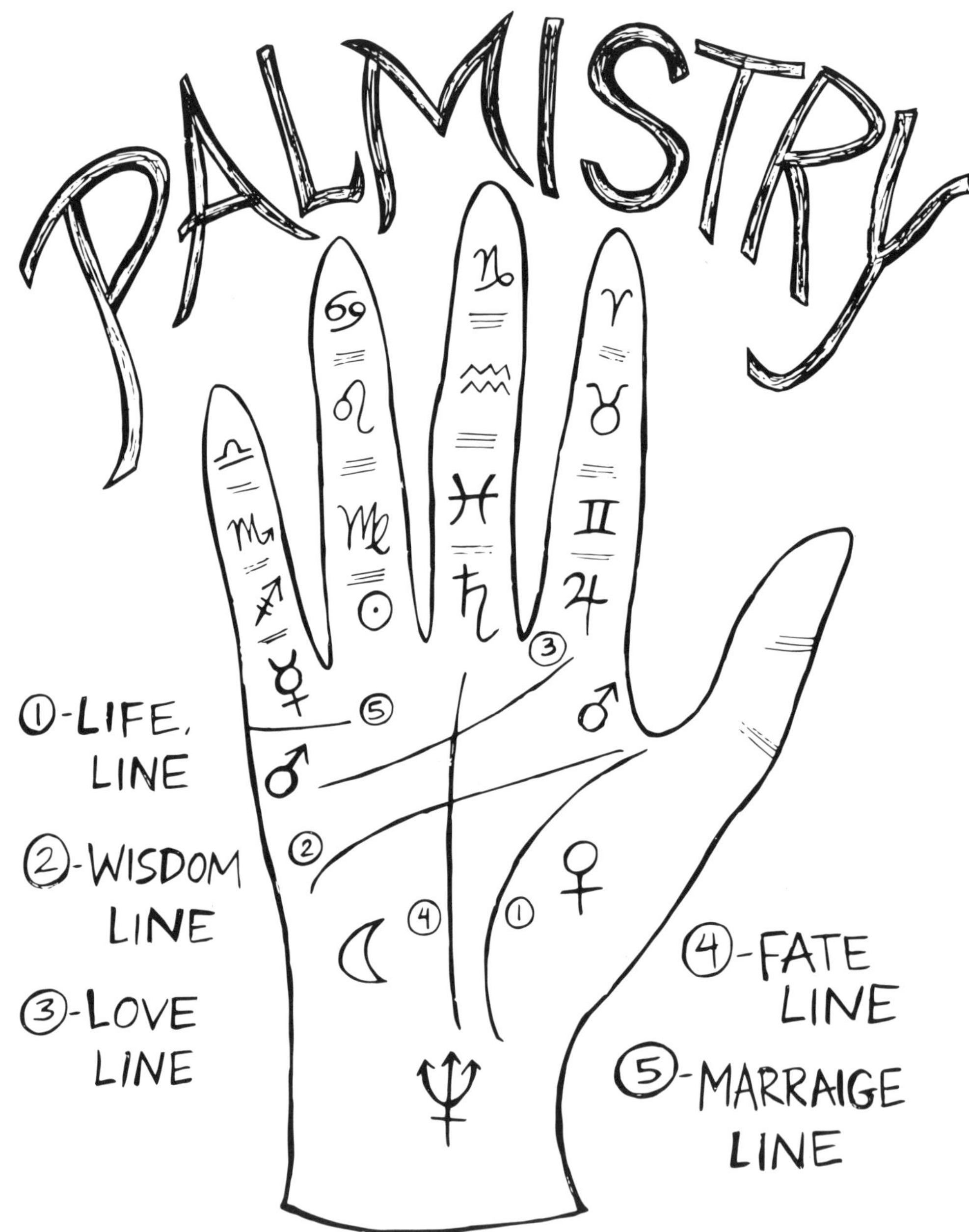

PALMISTRY
1-LIFE LINE
2-WISDOM LINE
3-LOVE LINE
4-FATE LINE
5-MARRAIGE LINE

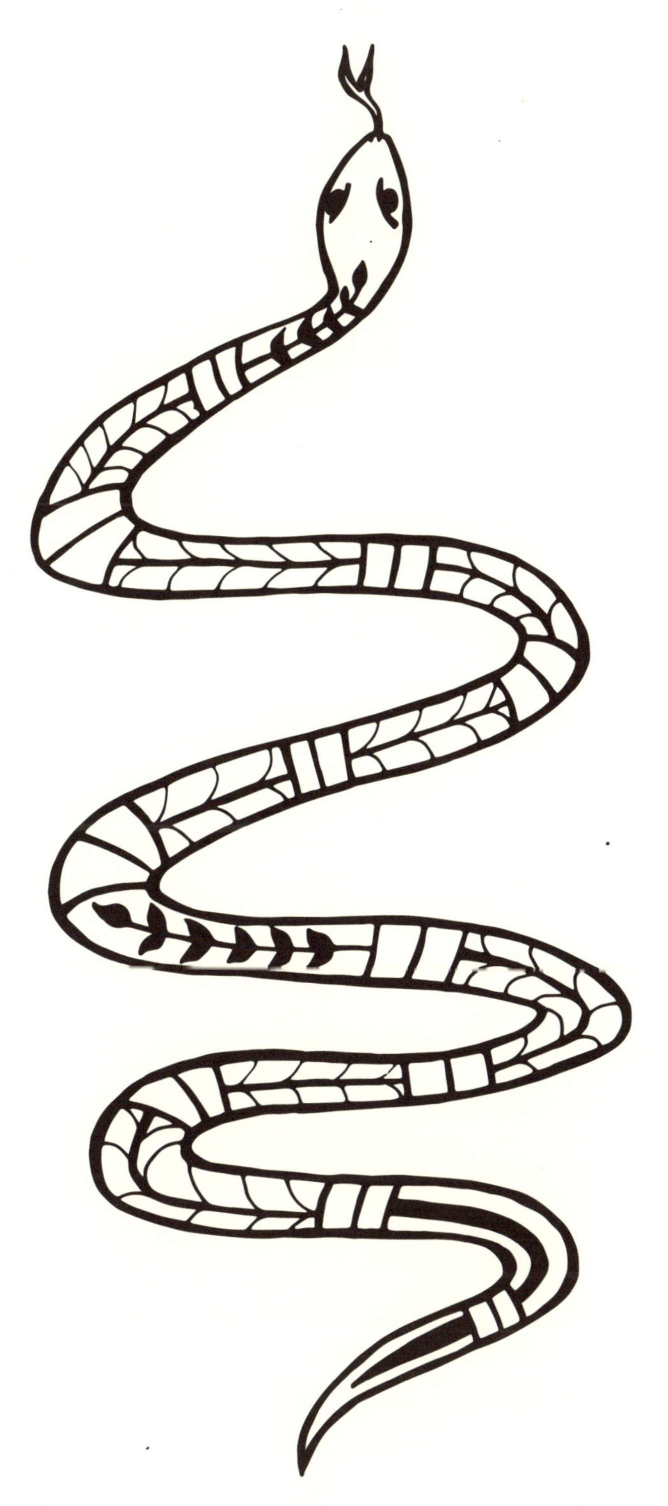

Candle Magick Colors

Red fire, energy, Sex, Passion

Orange Creativity, opportunity, Positivity

Yellow Communication, intelligence, genius

Green Prosperity, wealth, health, good luck

Blue Truth, wisdom, peace, angelic forces

Purple Divination, Psychic abilities, Empowerment

Pink Love, Romance, friendship, compassion

Brown Justice, grounding, earth/animal connections

Black Banishing, protection, remove hexes + negativity

White Purification, healing, blessings

Gold Success, wealth, Money, Good luck

Silver Intuition, healing, connection

Light/Dark Reversal, harmony, balance

·Spellwork·

Days of the Week

☉ Sunday

Success, Beauty, Health

☽ Monday

Healing, Intuition, Wisdom

♂ Tuesday

Courage, Strength, Protection

☿ Wednesday

Communication, travel, Job

♃ Thursday

Luck, Fortune, Harvest

♀ Friday

Romance, Sex, Friendship

♄ Saturday

Hope, Banishment, Service

Zodiac Signs

♈ Aries
♉ Taurus
♊ Gemini
♋ Cancer
♌ Leo
♍ Virgo
♎ Libra
♏ Scorpio
♐ Sagittarius
♑ Capricorn
♒ Aquarius
♓ Pisces

ASTR

OLOGY

Philosophy, + Travel

Sex, death, + Rebirth

8

7

Partnership

ES

6

Health + Service

5

Creativity + Children

Home

Planetary Symbols

☉ Sun
☽ Moon
☿ Mercury
♀ Venus
♂ Mars
♃ Jupiter
♄ Saturn
♅ Uranus
♆ Neptune
♇ Pluto
☊ North Node
☋ South Node
⚸ Lilith

I ask for all the effects
of my mistakes to be undone
in all directions of time,
and I now release all
guilt completely.

I affirm that I love my
true self, from top to
bottom, inside and out, with
grace, compassion, and tenderness,
forever and always.

I NOW CLEAR
IN ALL DIRECTIONS OF
TIME THE ENERGY THAT
WAS NEVER MINE TO
CARRY

I AM MAKING ROOM AND WELCOMING NEW ENERGY AND ALL FORMS OF ABUNDANCE IN GOOD HEALTH, JOY, LOVE, RESOURCES, CREATIVITY, AND MAGICK

I surrender all feelings of
and ask for support and
these energies into

POWER BACK

oubt, fear, or mistrust to source,
ivine alchemy to transmute
healing light for **all**.

Pagan Holiday

SAMHAIN · YULE · IMBOLC · OSTARA · BELTANE · LITHA · LUGHNASADH · MABON ·

SAMHAIN
OCTOBER 31st

YULE
WINTER SOLSTICE
DECEMBER 19–22

IMBOLC
February 1st

OSTARA
SPRING EQUINOX
MARCH 19–22

BELTANE
MAY 1st

LITHA
SUMMER SOLSTICE
JUNE 19–22

LUGHNASADH
AUGUST 1st

MABON
AUTUMN EQUINOX
SEPTEMBER 19–22

Wheel of the Year

TO BREAK SPELLS, CURSES, OR ENCHANTMENTS USED AGAINST OR TO CONTROL YOU REPEAT 9x's

THAT WHICH IS NOT ON MY BODY IS NOT OF MY BODY

Return to sender all energy sent here
Send it all back until I'm
energetically clear

If you sent me good will, I wish you no ill
If you wished for my doom,
I send back your gloom

Return to sender
All energy sent here
Send it all back until I'm
energetically clear

SPEAK IT INTO EXISTENCE

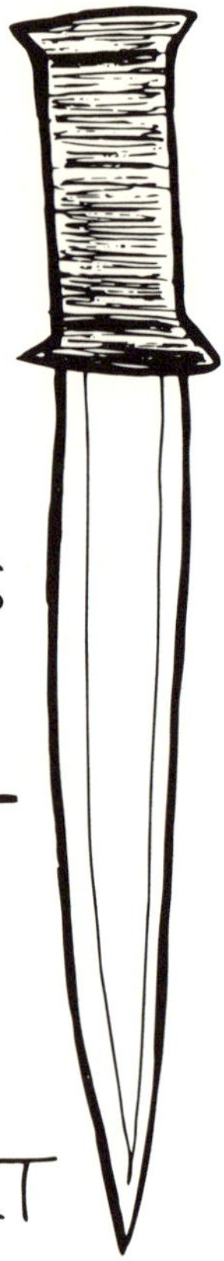

TAKE MY WISHES
TAKE MY FEARS
TAKE MY WORRY
BRING BACK THE YEARS
OF LOST CHILDREN
WHO HAD TO FIGHT
THE WISDOM EARNED
IN BLACKEND NIGHT
I RECLAIM MY HEART
THIS VERY HOUR
IF ANYONE DARE DIFFER
I WILL DEVOUR

10 SIGNS OF PSYCHIC ATTACK

~Negative Thoughts~

If you are normally positive and optimistic then suddenly find yourself sullen or pessimistic, you may be under psychic attack

~Aches, Pains, + Migraines~

If you are having these symptoms for no medical reason, you may be under psychic attack

~Drained Energy~

If you are wiped of physical energy with no changes to your diet, exercise, or sleep schedule you may be under psychic attack

~Nightmares~

If you are having repetative nightmares of being chased or intent of harm, you may be under psychic attack

~Repetitive or Obsessive thoughts~

Reoccuring thoughts of someone who is angry, jealous, envious, or bad mouthing you, then there is a chance you are being consciously or subconsciously psychically attacked

~Panic Attacks~

Sudden onset of anxiety or panic over small things, than you may be under psychic attack

~MEMORY + LACK OF CONCENTRATION~

Issues focusing or remembering for no reason or suddenly, you may be under psychic attack

~Sick Animals + Plants~

Animals + plants tend to take on negative energy especially if they are trying to protect you. If you have sick animals or dying plants you may be under psychic attack

~Carrion Insects + Animals~

If you are being inundated by bugs, animals, or birds inside or outside your home eating dead flesh or Questionable items, then you may be under psychic attack

~Depression + Thoughts of Suicide~

If you are suddenly depressed, are overcome with dark thoughts, or experiencing suicidal thoughts this can be a sign of psychic attack

7
6
5
4
3
2
1

THE 7 MAJOR EARTH CHAKRAS

1 - BASE - Mount SHASTA, CALIFORNIA
(alternatives: GRAND CANYON, SEDONA, BLACK MESA)

2 - SACRAL - LAKE Titicaca, SOUTH AMERICA
(alternatives: MACHU PICCHU, AMAZON RIVER)

3 - SOLAR PLEXUS - ULURA, AUSTRALIA

4 - HEART - GLASTONBURY, ENGLAND
(alternatives: River GANGES, INDIA)

5 - THROAT - Great Pyramid, EGYPT

6 - THIRD EYE - KUH-E MALEK SIAH, IRAN
(alternative: MOUNT FUJI, JAPAN)

7 - CROWN - MOUNT KAILASH, TIBET

A BLESSING

MAY the SUN ALWAYS BE AS
WARM AS YOUR HEART

WHILE THE WIND WHISPERS
SONGS OF KINDNESS IN YOUR
EARS

MAY YOUR FEET ALWAYS KISS
THE EARTH, AND FEEL HER
SUPPORTIVE EMBRACE

WHILE THE STARS REMIND YOU
that YOU ARE INFINITELY LOVED

don't borrow

pain from your

Future

I FORGIVE EVERYONE
FOR EVERYTHING
RIGHT NOW

I FORGIVE MYSELF
FOR EVERYTHING
RIGHT NOW

I ASK FOR FORGIVENESS
FOR EVERYTHING
RIGHT NOW

Crystal
Healing

INSIGHT + WISDOM

AMETHYST
CLEAR QUARTZ
LEMURIAN QUARTZ
MOLDAVITE
LIBYAN DESERT GLASS

Prosperity + Good Luck

CITRINE
PYRITE
MALACHITE
ADVENTURINE
LAPIS LAZULI
JADE

CLEARING,
PROTECTION,
+
GROUNDING

SELENITE
BLACK TOURMALINE
OBSIDIAN
JET
SMOKEY QUARTZ
SHUNGITE

CREATIVITY + CONFIDENCE

CARNELIAN
TIGER'S EYE
ORANGE CALCITE

HEALTH

RUTILATED QUARTZ
HEMATITE
BLOODSTONE
BLUE LACE AGATE
TURQUOISE
SERPENTINE

LOVE

ROSE QUARTZ
KUNZITE
MORGANITE
RUBY
GARNET

How to CLEANSE YOUR CRYSTALS

MOONLIGHT

LEAVE THEM IN MOONLIGHT, especially full moons

VISUALIZE + INTENTION

CLEAR THEM WITH VISUALIZATION + SPOKEN INTENTION

WATER

SUBMERGE THEM IN WATER OR HOLD UNDER RUNNING WATER

SMOKE

BATH THEM IN INCENSE OR SMUDGE SMOKE

SOIL

BURY THEM IN THE EARTH OVERNIGHT

SALT

SOAK THEM IN SALT WATER OVERNIGHT

OTHER CRYSTALS (SELENITE/CLEAR QUARTZ)

LAY THE CRYSTAL ON TOP OF THE OTHER ONE

MIND'S EYE BLISSFULLY CLOSED

MIND'S EYE BLASTED WIDE OPEN

PRAY
4
MAGIC

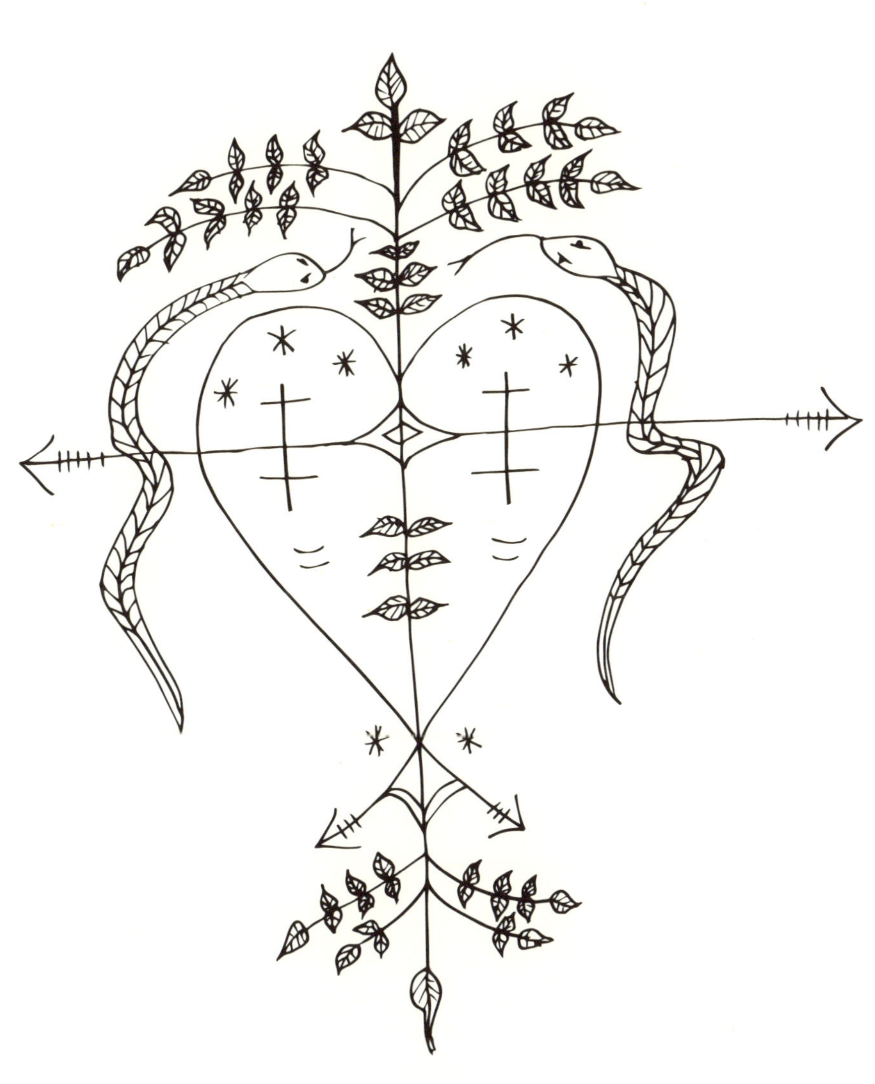

Self Love ♀ Jar

Materials:

A small mason jar w/lid, sugar, honey, sea salt, cinnamon, small tumbled rose quartz, dried rose petals, chocolate (a bar or some chips will do), and a pink candle.

What to do:

On a Friday (Venus Day) add your ingredients to your jar. As you add each ingredient, name one thing about yourself that you love. Close the jar by putting the lid on. Take your pink candle and fix it to the lid. Put the jar on your altar or some other place you will see it often. Light your candle and feel the love radiating back to you. Eat some of the chocolate and let your candle burn all the way to complete the spell.

Gone are the relationships that
want my energy, but do not respect
my time.

Gone are the wounded warriors that
cannot give love or cherish my
heart, body, and mind.

Gone are the time wasters and promise
breakers. There ain't no room for
any more space savers.

I'm calling in my Twin, my true
heart's desire,

My soulmate, my love, a true being
in their higher

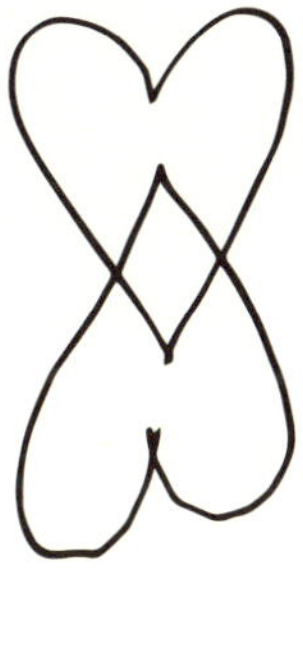

Mahal Kita

Go where

the Love is

Search FOR A MAGICAL MOTTO

MAGNA MAGIA

777

MAGNA SACERDOS MAGIA

THE SCARS MAY BE THERE
TO REMIND YOU
BUT THEY WILL NO
LONGER HAUNT YOU
OR HURT YOU

Write your wishes on bay leaves

when you burn them you release your wish to the

UNIVERSE

LOVE

HOME

JOY

PROSPERITY

Why does everything feel like an Initiation?

Luceo
Non
Uro

SHINE NOT BURN

I RELEASE ANY PAIN, TRAUMA,
ANGUISH, OR RESENTMENT
WITH ____________________
FROM THIS LIFE OR ANY
PAST LIFE

I RELEASE, CANCEL, CLEAR,
AND DELETE ANY VOWS, KARMIC
CONTRACTS WITH ____________________
FROM THIS LIFE OR ANY
PREVIOUS LIFETIMES

ALL IS FORGIVEN. ALL IS WELL.
WE ARE FREE TO BE HAPPY
AND THRIVING IN LOVE
AND SUCCESSFULLY

Keep the Faith

Even when it's really hard

If you are sincerely ready to let go,
the work may not be easy or fun,
but it is not impossible to do it.

I feel part of my purpose is to be
here to help people who are ready
to do the work, and be willing
to help themselves.

Ready to be honest with
themselves and show up, all
the way up.

If you cannot show up for you,
then neither can I.

STARING PROBLEMS

I don't fit in this world or maybe even
the next. I've never felt like I belonged.
I stand at the intersection of my ancestors.
Their pain, hurts, trauma, joy, and glory.
It means I have to heal all sides of the
wounds. I'm deep in colonizer, colonized,
oppressor, oppressed, slave owner, and the enslaved,
all coming together to resolve within me.
I have to reconcile the voices inside and out
that say "you have no business here, you do not
belong". This is the narrative and just part
of the story of my life and experience.
Fortunately it is just part. The rest of me
resides in a place of triumph that some will never
understand, because they have no idea what it
takes to come out of a swamp of despair and still
be breathing. Always on the border with one foot
in, and one foot out. Three near deaths will do that.
I know I am not the only one. There are
more like me. We are the Edge walkers.
We are the ones that will do what needs to
be done to end this cycle of pain, shame,
and blame. We will no longer be the
ones without a name.

We Summon Our
Courage
and Release the lies
+ ◇ +
We call back our
Power
and let our Spirits Rise

CASTING A CIRCLE

WILL AID YOU + PROTECT YOU FROM INTERFERING FORCES OR DISRUPTIVE ENERGIES

IT ALSO CREATES SACRED SPACE TO INVITE IN THE ELEMENTS, GUIDES, AND HELPFUL ALLIES

- BEFORE YOU BEGIN CLEANSE THE SPACE WITH SMOKE OR SOUND
- USE A WAND, ATHAME, OR TWO FINGERS TO MARK OUT THE CIRCLE
- TURN IN A CLOCKWISE MOTION TO EACH DIRECTION (BEGINNING WITH NORTH) TO SUMMON THE ELEMENTS INTO THE CIRCLE

NORTH · EAST · SOUTH · WEST · ABOVE · BELOW

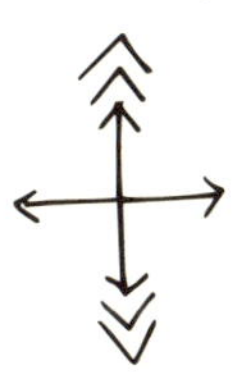

- NOW INVITE IN APPROPRIATE GUIDES, ANCESTORS, OR DEITIES
- DECLARE YOUR PETITION OR INTENTIONS
- UPON COMPLETION OF YOUR SPELLWORK THANK THE DEITIES, ANCESTORS, AND EACH DIRECTION AND ELEMENTS INVOKED IN A COUNTER CLOCKWISE MOTION
- WHEN FINISHED STATE "THE CIRCLE IS NOW OPEN"

YOUR ALTAR IS A PERSONAL AND SACRED SPACE
HONOR YOUR ANCESTORS, COMMUNE WITH YOUR
MAGICAL TOOLS. IT DOES NOT MATTER THE SIZE
KEEPING THIS SPACE TIDY AND AS A PLACE OF
ALTAR IF YOU LIKE. SOME DEITIES DO NOT LIKE
WANT TO DEDICATE AN ALTAR TO JUST YOUR ANCESTORS
HERE ARE SOME SUGGESTED (BUT NOT REQUIRED)

INCENSE, PHOTOGRAPHS, DRAWINGS OR
CAULDRON, WAND, PENTACLE,

FOR YOU TO PRAY, MEDITATE, PERFORM SPELLWORK,
GUIDES, INVITE IN ASSISTANCE, AND KEEP YOUR
OR HOW ELABORATE YOU MAKE IT. THIS IS UP TO YOU.
RESPECT IS KEY. YOU CAN HAVE MORE THAN ONE
COHABITATING WITH EACH OTHER, OR PERHAPS YOU
THAT IS PERFECTLY FINE AND WHATEVER YOU PREFER
ITEMS TO INCLUDE ON YOUR ALTAR SPACE...

STATUE FIGURES, CANDLES, CHALICE, ATHAME,

OR SACRED SYMBOL

Speak friend and enter

Pray Hard

Sometimes it's all you can do. Pray not only for yourself. Pray for all the living, the winged ones, standing people, two legged, four legged, those that walk, crawl, swim, and fly. Pray for those that cannot speak, have no or not found their voice. Pray for solutions that bring healing. Pray for relief from pain, trauma, and discomfort. Pray for healing and most of all for understanding. May all that we intend be right and good. May the short fuses light the way, but not burn the bridges to forgiveness. May we all do the best we can. Then in the space between We Pray... and We Pray Hard

HEARTBREAK + RECOVERY

YOUR HEART BROKE SO IT WOULD REFORM AND BE BIGGER. WALK PROUDLY WITH THIS STRANGE NEW SHAPE IT HAS BECOME. YOUR SCARS, WOUNDS REPAIRED, AND LAYERS OF DIFFERENTIATING COLOR SHOW THE WORLD THAT YOU TOOK A CHANCE. YOU LOVED DEEP, YOU LOVED RECKLESSLY. YOU OPENED YOURSELF TO THE WONDERS AND MAGIC OF THE WORLD AROUND YOU. YOU SHAMELESSLY ADORED SOMEONE OR SOMETHING OUT OF PURITY. IT'S TIME TO DO IT AGAIN. TIME TO BARE YOUR SOUL, AND WITNESS BREAKING THE GLASS CEILING THAT LIMITS WHAT YOU ARE CAPABLE OF. I CHALLENGE YOU TO NOT RISTRICT YOUR LOVE THIS TIME AROUND. DON'T WAIT FOR SOMEONE ELSE TO SHOW YOU FIRST. I DARE YOU TO GIVE IT MORE THAN YOU HAVE BEFORE. BE FEARLESS, BE HONEST, AND BE FREE

How to alienate friends and Napalm people

DO YOU EVER FEEL LIKE YOU HAVE A HARD TIME ASKING FOR WHAT YOU NEED? PEOPLE WANT ME TO COMMUNICATE BUT WHEN I DO IT BECOMES A PROBLEM. I'M REALLY JUST LONELY. I FEEL SO MUCH ALL THE TIME AND HAVE SO MANY PUTTING THEIR STUFF ON ME THEN ACCUSE ME OF BEING DRAMATIC. MAGIC IS IN MY ABILITY TO TRANSLATE HEARTBREAK INTO RECOVERY, BUT THE RIDE CAN BE BUMPY. I PRAY WE ALL CAN LEARN HOW TO ASK FOR WHAT WE NEED AND RECEIVE SUPPORT.

sulphur

saltpetre

Black Salt

-Recipe-

* Course Sea Salt (2lb bag)
* Activated Charcoal (4 tablespoons)
* Camphor Essential Oil (6-7 drops)
* Lavender Essential Oil (8-9 drops)

Blend all items together and store in a cool and dry place

Do Not Eat or Ingest!

LEAD

ANTIMONY

AMMONIA

ALUMEN

ARSENIC OLIVE OIL ARSENIC

Black Salt can be

used for energy clearing, protection magic, ritual work, and as an altar offering. You can add it to your bath to clear your auric field. You can place it in window sills or across the threshold of your front door. You can place some in a dish on your night stand to help ward off nightmares.

BRASS

SALT LEAD SALT

COPPER MORTAR VINEGAR

Happiness
Luck
Health
Good Fortune

I DON'T HAVE TO BE SICK
TO CHANGE

I DON'T HAVE TO BE BAD
TO CHANGE

I DON'T NEED TO HAVE
CATASTROPHIC EVENTS
OR
DRAMA TO CHANGE

ABRACADABRA
ABRACADABR
ABRACADAB
ABRACADA
ABRACAD
ABRACA
ABRAC
ABRA
ABR
AB
A

Transmutation

Transmutation

IF YOU HAVE FOUND YOUR WAY HERE TO THESE PAGES, THEN I'M PRETTY CERTAIN THAT YOU HAVE HEARD THE SMALL VOICE BECKONING YOU CLOSER, INVITING YOU TO FORGET WHAT YOU THINK YOU KNOW, AND TO REMEMBER WHAT YOU HAVE FORGOTTEN. SO HOW DO WE CALL BACK OUR MAGIC, POWER, AND WISDOM? HOW DO WE RECLAIM OUR DIVINITY AND MAGICAL BIRTHRIGHT? THERE ARE MANY THINGS IN THIS WORLD THAT WILL TRY TO DISTRACT YOU FROM DOING SO. IT COULD BE OLD FAMILIAL PATTERNS, SYSTEMIC TRAUMA, FINANCIAL FEAR, GOVERNMENTAL OPPRESSION, AND DEEPLY ROOTED PAST AND PRESENT LIFE HABITS OF PERSECUTION SURVIVAL THAT KEEP YOU SMALL. WE ALL HAVE THESE CONNECTIONS EVEN IF INDIRECTLY. THE BIGGEST THING WITH TRAUMA EVEN IF YOU DIDN'T EXPERIENCE IT, BUT YOUR RELATIVE EXPERIENCED IT, IT IS NOW SCIENTIFICALLY PROVEN TO BE PASSED DOWN IN YOUR DNA. SO YOU DEAL WITH IT, EVEN IF IT'S DORMANT. MANY OF US ARE JUST BEGINNING TO UNDERSTAND OUR OWN SURVIVAL HAS BEEN ROOTED IN STAYING HIDDEN.

RECLAIMING YOUR MAGIC IS NO SIMPLE TASK. IT IS IN FACT A JOURNEY. ONE THAT WILL REQUIRE YOU TO MAKE NEW DISCOVERIES, AND UNCOVER DEEPLY HIDDEN TRUTHS. YOU WILL ALSO MAKE TERRIBLE AND WONDERFUL MISTAKES. ONES WHERE YOU WILL LEARN THE VALUE OF YOUR SPIRIT, AND HOW TO FIND VALUE IT HAS. THE PAIN AND THE MISTAKES ARE WHERE YOU MEASURE RESPONSIBILITY. RECLAIMING YOUR MAGIC REQUIRES YOU TO ACKNOWLEDGE YOUR POWER AND ACCEPT YOURSELF FOR WHERE YOU ARE. IT REQUIRES BRAVERY TO ADMIT WHERE YOU SCREWED UP AND WHAT YOU WILL DO TO AMEND IT. THIS PATH IS NOT FOR THE FAINT OF HEART OR THE SURFACE INTERACTION. IT IS ABOUT A WILLINGNESS TO EXPLORE THE VAST ENORMITY OF YOUR OWN BEING AND BEING COURAGEOUS ENOUGH TO CLAIM RESPONSIBILITY. THE BIGGER THE LIGHT, THE BIGGER THE SHADOW IS CAST, AND ALL THAT WAS HIDDEN IS NOW AVAILABLE FOR ALL (NOT JUST THE SELF) TO SEE. THERE WILL BE NO DENYING WHAT HAS FELT LACKING WHEN YOU REALIZE WHAT WAS MISSING IN THE FIRST PLACE, SO I CAUTION YOU, DO NOT SAY THIS NEXT PART ALOUD UNLESS YOU ARE ABSOLUTELY CERTAIN THAT YOU ARE READY, BECAUSE ONCE YOU OPEN THIS DOOR, THERE IS NO GOING BACK TO A PLACE OF KNOWING NOTHING.

⟶

I AM NOW READY
TO RECLAIM MY
WISDOM
POWER
BLESSINGS
GIFTS
UNIQUE BEAUTY
+
DIVINE BIRTHRIGHT

Mommy
Issues

LADIES CURE YOUR HPV NATURALLY

*BE SURE IT'S STRUCTURED SILVER

- MIX 3oz SILVER WITH 3oz DISTILLED WATER
- PUMP INTO VAGINA AND HOLD FOR 30 MINS
- REPEAT 3-5 DAYS
- UP YOUR ANTIOXIDANTS
- TAKE PROBIOTICS
- REDUCE SUGAR
- PLEASE BE ADVISED... THIS IS NOT A CURE ALL
- GET TESTED FREQUENTLY

This too
shall pass...

TODAY I RECLAIM MY BIRTHRIGHT TO
ENJOY THIS PHYSICAL BODY, MY VESSLE,
MY SPIRIT HOUSE, MY TEMPLE.

I RELEASE ANY FEAR, SHAMING, HIDING,
DISGUST, OR NEGATIVE PERCEPTIONS AROUND
MY BODY. WHETHER THEY ARE MINE IN ORIGIN,
PASSED DOWN GENERATIONALLY FROM MY MOTHER,
FATHER, FAMILY OF ORIGIN, COMMUNITY, OR SOCIETY.

I CALL MY POWER BACK FROM EVERY SITUATION
I CREATED TO CONTINUE THE CYCLE OF SELF
HARM, EATING DISORDERS, AND SHAME.

I LET GO OF THE RERUNS AND REPEATED
PATTERNS OF BODY DYSMORPHIA AND HATEFUL
SELF TALK.

I CALL BACK THE DIVINE IN ME.
I CALL BACK MY RIGHT TO BE HAPPY,
TO BE FREE,
IN MY CURRENT BODY.

Letter Spells

You can use the method when the lines of communication are blocked, when you want to release yourself from a relationship or situation, and the traditional means of closure are not available.

When you write your letter, you address the person or situation on all levels. Your feelings are attached. It's important to remember to include everything you are feeling and have felt for the person or situation. EVERYTHING. Not just the frustration or the sadness, but the good times, happiness and gratitude as well. The pen to paper represents the elements of air and earth. Your next step is to use the element of fire, and burn the letter (you might want to do this outside in a fire safe place). Then the final element to join in is water. You can either pour water over the ashes or flush the ashes down the toilet.

THE ELEMENTS CREATE AN ALCHEMY TO IGNITE THE ENERGY OF THE MESSAGE IN THE LETTER. THE POWER OF WORD, COMBINED WITH INTENT, AND THE ELEMENTS CAN PRODUCE DIRECT AND SWIFT RESULTS. REMEMBER TO USE YOUR WORDS AND MAGIC RESPONSIBLY. THEY HAVE POWER IN THEM.

Never Give Up!

THE FAERYSTAR

AKA THE ELVEN STAR

A GIFT FROM THE FAERIES TO HUMANITY. A BRIDGE OF KNOWLEDGE AND UNDERSTANDING BETWEEN THE TWO. THE SEVEN POINTED STAR SERVES AS A GATEWAY TO THE FAERIE REALM. IT IS ALSO SYMBOLIC OF THE SEVEN MANIFESTATIONS OF THE HIGHER SELF. THIS IS A POWERFUL SYMBOL! ONLY USE IT WILL REVERANCE, RESPECT, AND TRUE UNDERSTANDING OF WHAT AND WHO YOU ARE INVITING IN.

DO NOT PISS OFF THE FAERIES!

7 POINTS REPRESENT

POWER – UNCONDITIONAL LOVE – INTELLIGENCE
HARMONY – SCIENCE – DEVOTION – MAGIC

NOT EVERYONE IS GOING TO LIKE YOU, AND THAT'S OK

TO STOP SOMEONE FROM GOSSIPING ABOUT YOU, BULLYING OR HARASSING YOU, OR GIVING YOU A HARD TIME

FREEZER SPELL

—WHAT YOU NEED—

A FREEZER BAG WITH A ZIPPER SEAL, A PEN, AND PIECE OF PAPER

—WHAT TO DO—

WRITE THE NAME OF THE PERSON HARASSING YOU ON A PIECE OF PAPER AND PLACE IT IN THE ZIPPER BAG. FILL THE BAG WITH WATER, AND THEN SEAL IT. PLACE THE BAG IN YOUR FREEZER, AND AS THE PERSON'S NAME FREEZES UP, THEY SHOULD LEAVE YOU BE.

—TO COMPLETE—

WHEN YOU FEEL THE SPELL IS COMPLETE REMOVE THE BAG AND TOSS THE BAG IN A PUBLIC TRASH.

PERSONALLY I'M NOT A FAN OF PUTTING LOVE SPELLS ON SPECIFIC PEOPLE. IT DOES NOT FEEL MORALLY UPRIGHT TO TRY AND MANIPULATE ANOTHER'S FEELINGS. HOWEVER I DO SUPPORT LOVE BASED SPELLS THAT HELP ESTABLISH RECIPRICAL AND FAVORABLE ROMANCE IN YOUR LIFE WHILE ALSO RESPECTING THE FREE WILL AND AUTHENTIC CONNECTION OF ANOTHER. HERE ARE SOME SUGGESTIONS AND POTENTIAL INTENTION SETTING IDEAS TO INVITE HARMONIOUS CONNECTION IN YOUR LIFE WITHOUT IMPOSING YOUR WILL ON ANOTHER...

♥ WORKING YOUR SPELL ON A FRIDAY (VENUS DAY) BETWEEN THE NEW AND FULL MOON

♥ FLOWERS FOR YOURSELF, ALTAR, AS AN OFFERING PINK AND/OR RED

- ♥ SWEET ALMOND OIL
- ♥ INCENSE IF YOU DESIRE (ROSE, PATCHOULI, AMBER)
- ♥ 2 CANDLES (PINK-(LOVE) RED-(PASSION))
- ♥ HONEY OR SUGAR
- ♥ PEN, PAPER, AND WRITING UTENSIL
- ♥ ROMANTIC MUSIC IF YOU DESIRE

YOU CAN USE ALL OR ONE OR EVEN NONE OF THESE ITEMS TO CREATE THE VIBE FOR YOUR WORK. WHAT'S IMPORTANT IS YOUR FOCUS AND INTENTION. BEFORE ANY SPELL SET THE TONE BY CASTING A CIRCLE. PUT ON YOUR MUSIC. LIGHT YOUR INCENSE. TAKE YOUR CANDLE(S) AND ANOINT THEM WITH THE ALMOND OIL. THEN EITHER ROLL THEM IN SUGAR, OR LEAVE A PINCH OF SUGAR OR OFFERING OF HONEY ON YOUR ALTAR. WRITE OUT 21 TRAITS OF YOUR IDEAL LOVE MATCH, LIGHT YOUR CANDLE(S) THEN READ YOUR LIST ALOUD. LEAVE YOUR LIST ON YOUR ALTAR. WHEN THE CANDLE(S) HAVE BURNED COMPLETELY TUCK YOUR LIST AWAY

ASH
APPLE
ALDER
ASPEN
AVOCADO
BAY LAUREL
BIRCH
BODHI
CEDAR
CHASTE TREE
CHERRY
CYPRESS
DRAGON'S BLOOD
ELDER
ELM
FIG
HAWTHORN
HOLLY
JACARANDA
JOSHUA TREE
JUNIPER
LEMON
MAPLE
OAK
PALM
PALO SANTO
PINE
PINYON
REDWOOD
ROWAN
YEW

AS FOR WORTHINESS...

I WOULD TELL YOU, YOU ARE WORTHY!

YOU ARE WORTHY OF A PARTNER IF YOU DESIRE. A PARTNER THAT LOVES YOU UNCONDITIONALLY. SOMEONE THAT UNDERSTANDS AND VALUES ALL THAT YOU DO FOR YOURSELF TO INSPIRE POSITIVE CHANGE, SUPPORT, AND GROWTH IN OTHERS, AND THE WORLD AROUND YOU! A PARTNER THAT WANTS TO GROW AND EVOLVE TOGETHER. A DIVINE COMPLIMENT THAT MAKES YOU FEEL SAFE, PROVIDED FOR AND LIKE THE SEXIEST, MOST BELOVED CREATURE WHO WALKS THIS EARTH.

VAN VAN OIL

A WONDERFUL OIL USED TO CLEAR OUT BAD LUCK, INVITE IN POSITIVE EXPERIENCES, AND COUNTERACT ANY ILL EFFECTS OF A MERCURY RETROGRADE CYCLE. USE TO ANOINT AND EMPOWER SACRED OBJECTS, CANDLES, ON YOUR BODY, AND EVEN A FEW DROPS IN A FLOOR WASH TO REFRESH THE SPIRIT OF YOUR HOME.

BLEND THE FOLLOWING ESSENTIAL OILS; LEMONGRASS, CITRONELLA, PALMAROSA, + VETIVER INTO A SWEET ALMOND OIL BASE

IF YOU WANT TO GIVE YOUR OIL A "CAN DO" KICK ADD A SMALL PIECE OF PYRITE (FOOL'S GOLD) OR CARNELIAN TO ENHANCE THE POWER OF THE OIL.

The Money I need the Universe will send, opening the path to wealth without end.

A SIMPLE MONEY DRAW SPELL
TO DO ON THE FULL MOON

—WHAT YOU NEED—

A GREEN CANDLE
A WHITE CANDLE
SWEET ALMOND OIL
POWDERED CINNAMON

—WHAT TO DO—

- ANOINT THE CANDLES WITH THE OIL, WHILE DOING SO VISUALIZE THE WEALTH YOU WANT TO RECEIVE. SPRINKLE THE CINNAMON ON THE CANDLES.
- PLACE THE CANDLES ON YOUR ALTAR, 5 INCHES APART.
- LIGHT THE CANDLES AND RECITE THE FOLLOWING

"MONEY MONEY COME TO ME
IN ABUNDANCE TIMES 3
MAY I BE BLESSED UP IN THE BEST WAYS
WITH HARM TO NONE WHEN IN ROUTE TODAY
THIS I ACCEPT SO MOTE IT BE
BRING ME THE MONEY, 3 Xs 3"

- MOVE THE WHITE CANDLE 1" CLOSER TO THE GREEN CANDLE AS YOU CHANT.
- AFTER CHANTING EXTINGUISH THE FLAMES.
- REPEAT THIS SPELL FOR 5 DAYS, EACH DAY MOVING THE WHITE CANDLE CLOSER TO THE GREEN. VISUALIZING THE WEALTH YOU DESIRE.
- ON THE FIFTH DAY, WHEN THE CANDLES TOUCH, YOUR SPELL IS FINISHED. LET THE CANDLES BURN UNTIL THERE IS NOTHING LEFT.

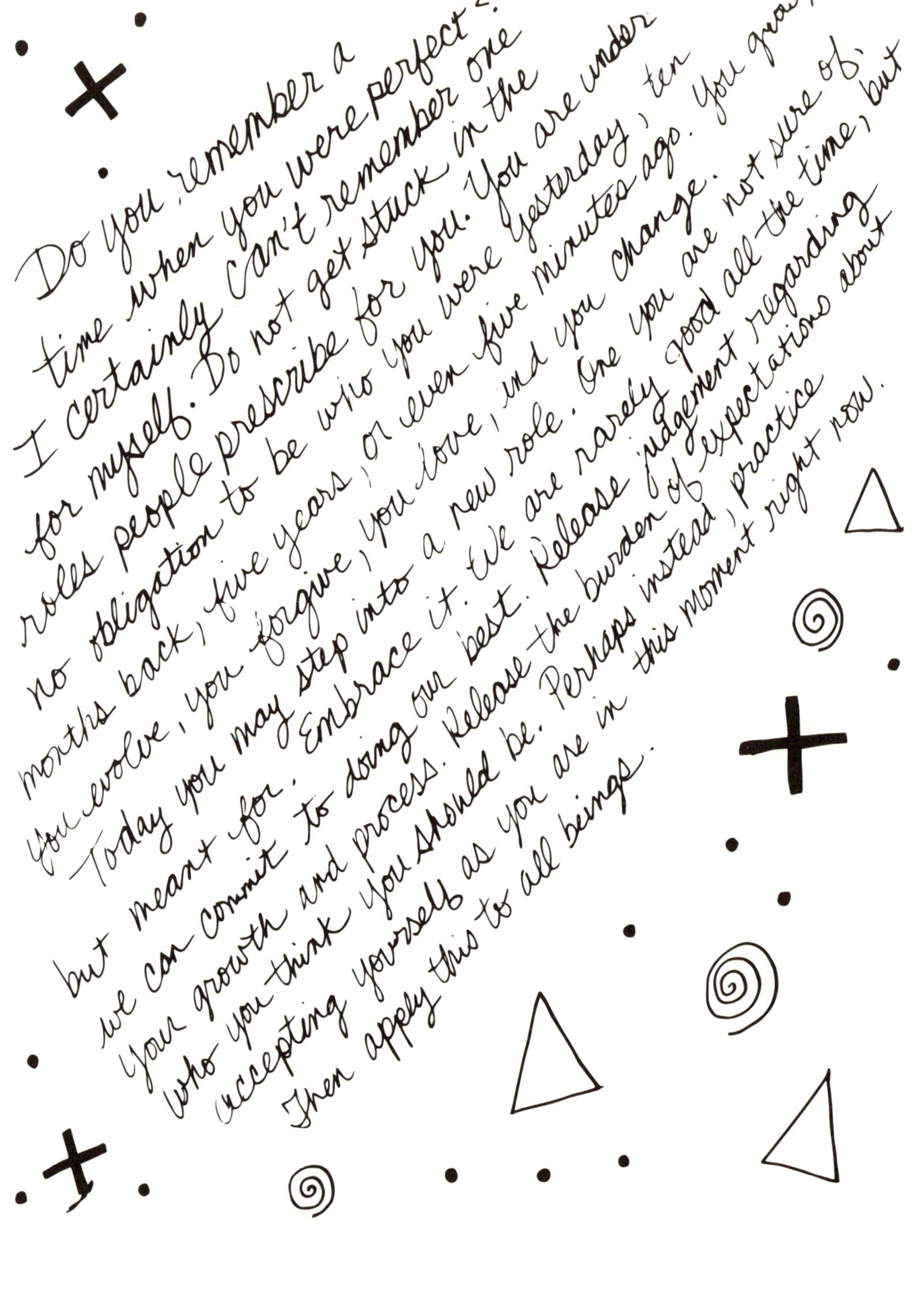
Do you remember a
time when you were perfect?.
I certainly can't remember one
for myself. Do not get stuck in the
roles people prescribe for you. You are under
no obligation to be who you were yesterday, ten
months back, five years, or even five minutes ago. You grow,
you evolve, you forgive, you love, and you change.
Today you may step into a new role. One you are not sure of,
but meant for. Embrace it. We are rarely good all the time, but
we can commit to doing our best. Release judgement regarding
your growth and process. Release the burden of expectations about
who you think you should be. Perhaps instead, practice
accepting yourself as you are in this moment right now.
Then apply this to all beings.

MOON Phases

NEW MOON
WAXING CRESCENT
FIRST QUARTER
WAXING GIBBOUS
FULL MOON
WANING GIBBOUS
LAST QUARTER
WANING CRESCENT

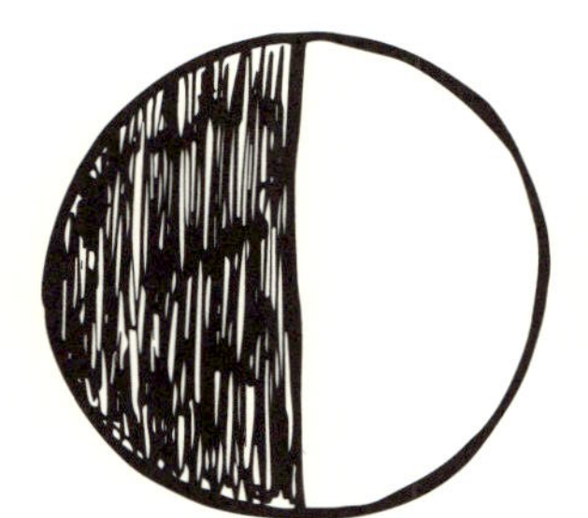

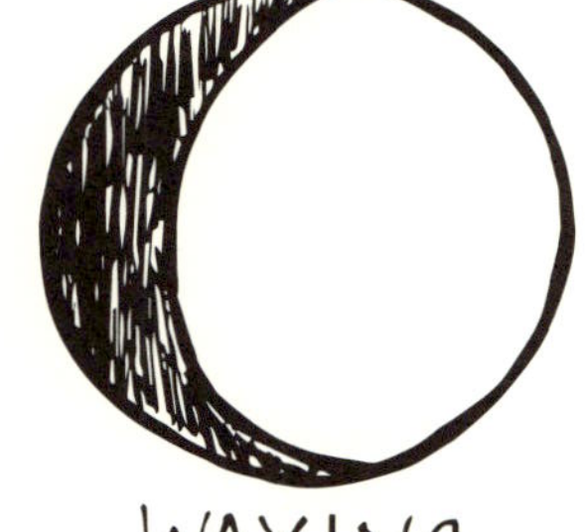

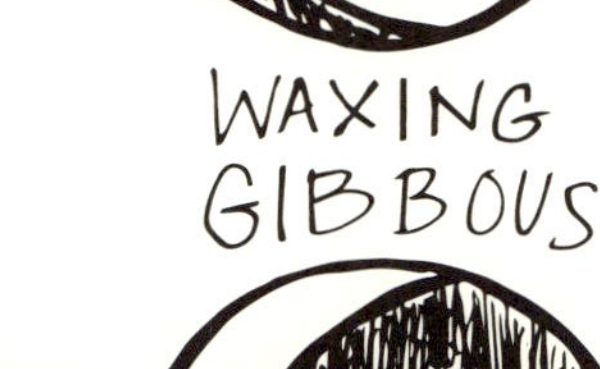

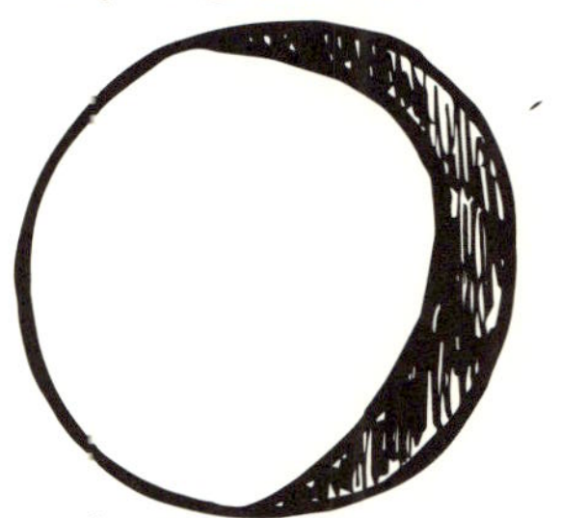

MAY THE TEARS I CRY
CLEANSE MY SPIRIT

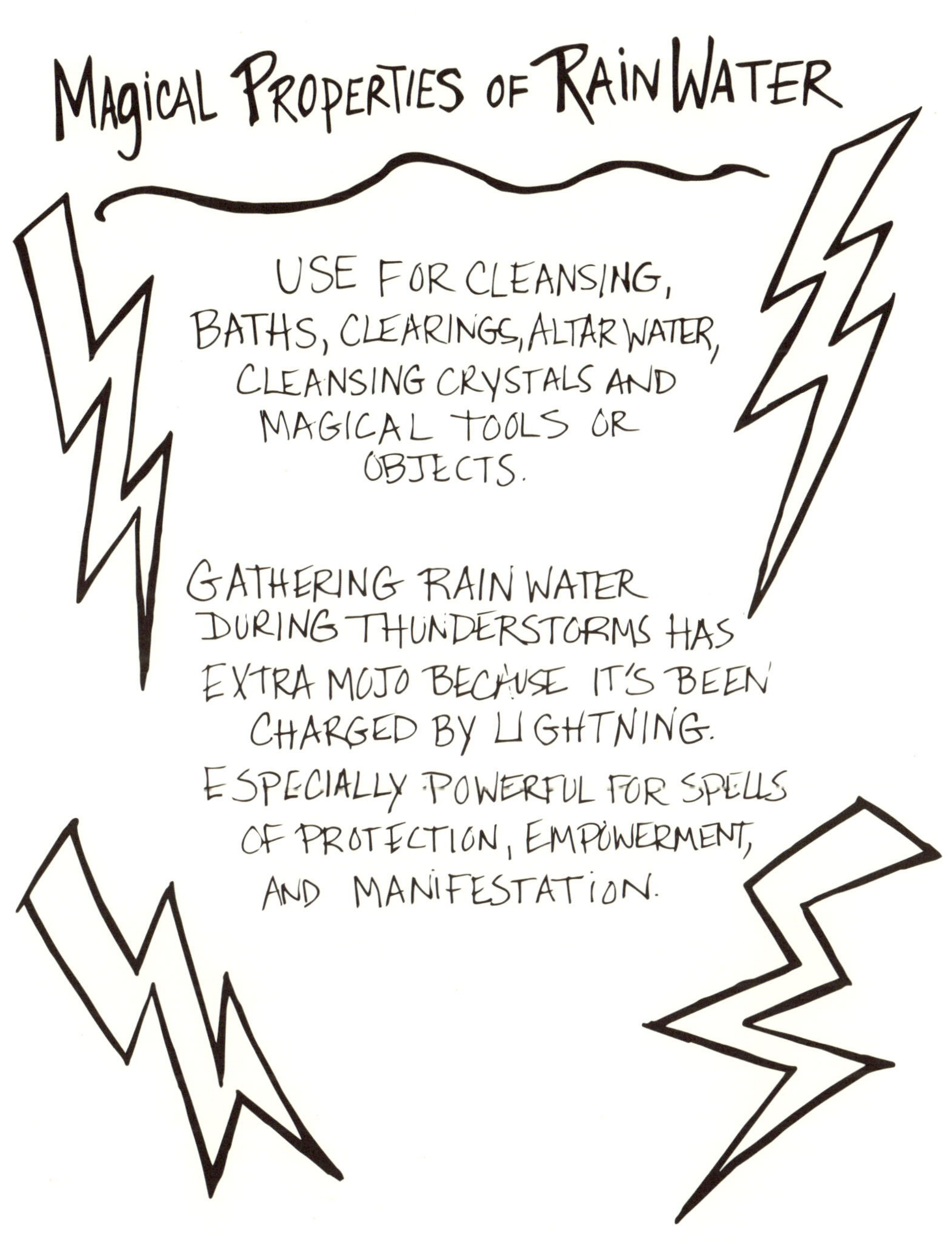
MAGICAL PROPERTIES OF RAIN WATER
USE FOR CLEANSING, BATHS, CLEARINGS, ALTAR WATER, CLEANSING CRYSTALS AND MAGICAL TOOLS OR OBJECTS.
GATHERING RAIN WATER DURING THUNDERSTORMS HAS EXTRA MOJO BECAUSE IT'S BEEN CHARGED BY LIGHTNING. ESPECIALLY POWERFUL FOR SPELLS OF PROTECTION, EMPOWERMENT, AND MANIFESTATION.

– Open letter of Encouragement –

Darling, if I can say I have been blessed by anything, it would be by the stupid sense of ambition to always do what I am told that I cannot, and to go after what I was told I would never be able to experience. My motivation in life has always been to rebel against these sentiments. To prove that you can make a difference and that it doesn't matter where you come from. Often misundersto Some diagnose me with commitment issues, or worse. They accuse me of being lost or assume I am just wanting things I cannot have. None of this is true or accurate.

I want to live a BIG LIFE. I refuse to live small. This may Lead to changes in my outer appearance, different circles o groups/friends/community, abruptly leaving scenarios, trave talk, and study of uncomfortable subjects, or abandoning ideas I have outgrown. So in this way I am always exploring, wandering, taking risks, and going on an adventure. I want to experience all I can while in this physical body, and while I have the energy.

I encourage you all to do the same. Be Forewarned though, not everyone will be comfortable. They will challenge your drive, your authenticity, and audacity. Do it anyway. Let any challenge motivate and fuel you to reach higher and break the proverbial glass ceiling (even if it's just in your mind).

I am here to show you that it can be done and done again. Then when you feel alone on your path remind yourself that you didn't do it for anyone else. You kept your word to yourself. Let go of expectations for others to get it right away, or to even follow suit. They are not your responsibility. You give love, honor, and respect to others on their path, but continue on minding your own business.

There will be days where it won't seem worth it, and you are longing for company. You might settle for bad behavior + shitty relationships that compromise the promise you made to yourself. But there will be a moment when it's very clear. You must walk away and no longer support throwing salt on wounds that don't allow you to heal. It will be sad, there will be grief, but you will move on, and you will get through this. I swear you will.

Love,

Marcella

KITCHEN WITCHERY

COURAGE
PEPPER
BASIL
HORSERADISH
NETTLE
YARROW

SUCCESS
BAY
ROSEMARY
SAFFRON
DILL
GINGER
LEMON
MINT
BASIL

LOVE
VANILLA
CINNAMON
CORIANDER
LAVENDER

PEACE
MARJORAM
MINT
CLARY SAGE
LEMON BALM
CHAMOMILE

HAPPINESS
MINT
FEVERFEW
CALENDULA
CHAMOMILE
NUTMEG
ORANGE
LEMON

LUCK
ALLSPICE
COMFREY
NUTMEG
BAY

TRAVEL
CARAWAY
FENNEL
MUSTARD
PARSLEY
COMFREY

PROTECTION
ANGELICA
BASIL
GARLIC
PEPPERMINT
PEPPER
CLOVE
MUGWORT
CARAWAY

MONEY
BASIL
DILL
CINNAMON
GINGER
MINT
PARSLEY

INSIGHT
ORANGE
SAGE
LEMONGRASS
MUGWORT

HEALTH
ALLSPICE
ANGELICA
HYSSOP
GARLIC
CALENDULA
TUMERIC
ROSEMARY

BITCH BE GONE

+BANISHING SPELL+

USE TO RID YOURSELF OF A PESTERING BULLY, AN EX, ENEMY, OR BAD PERSONAL HABIT

PART I – BANISHING OIL

SESAME OIL (BASE), BLACK PEPPER, GARLIC CLOVE OR POWDER, DRIED HOT PEPPER, SMALL JAR OR BOTTLE WITH TIGHT LID, AND GLOVES

- WEARING THE GLOVES COMBINE ALL INGREDIENTS IN JAR
- SEAL AND SHAKE, STORE IN DARK COOL PLACE FOR 2 WEEKS

PART II – SPELLWORK

1 BLACK CANDLE, NAIL, BANISHING OIL, GLOVES

- CARVE THE NAME OR BAD HABIT YOU ARE TRYING TO BE RID OF FROM THE TOP DOWNWARDS TOWARDS THE BOTTOM OF THE CANDLE WITH THE NAIL ↓
- WEARING GLOVES ANOINT THE CANDLE WITH THE OIL
- LIGHT THE CANDLE AND SAY OUTLOUD

  "BITCH BE GONE, BITCH GO AWAY.
  YOU'RE NOT WELCOME HERE ANOTHER DAY"
- LET BURN COMPLETELY

DIVINE

ANOINTING OIL

A BLEND I CREATED TO HELP CLEAR MY ENERGY IN BETWEEN TAROT READINGS FOR CLIENTS. IT IS MEANT TO HONOR YOUR SPIRIT, CLEAR YOUR BODY + MIND, WHILE KEEPING YOUR HEART OPEN TO YOUR OWN DIVINITY.

TO MAKE, YOU WILL NEED TO BLEND THE FOLLOWING INGREDIENTS. DON'T FORGET TO MAGICALLY CHARGE THIS OIL WITH YOUR INTENTION.

BASE: FRACTURED COCONUT OIL

ESSENTIAL OILS: PALO SANTO, TOBACCO, LAVENDER, FRANKINCENSE, + CEDARWOOD

SYNTHETIC: AMBROXAN (OIL OR CRYSTALS)

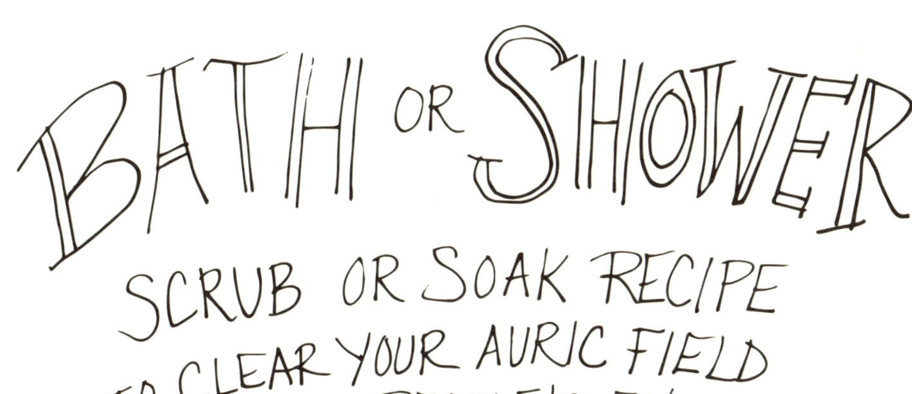

BATH OR SHOWER

SCRUB OR SOAK RECIPE TO CLEAR YOUR AURIC FIELD OF OTHER PEOPLE'S ENERGY

COMBINE A BLEND OF COARSE AND FINE SEA SALT, ROSE PETALS, SWEET ALMOND OIL, FRESH LAVENDER OR LAVENDER ESSENTIA OIL, SWEET ORANGE ESSENTIAL OIL, AND/OR ROSEMARY OIL.

ADD 1 CUP TO YOUR BATH TO SOAK OR SCRUB YOUR BODY WITH A PALM SIZE AMOUNT.

AS YOU DO YOU CAN RECITE...

I NOW RELEASE ANY PERSON OR ANYTHING I HAVE CONNECTED TO ON THIS DAY. WE ARE ALL FREE TO BE ON OUR WAY.

Lodestone IS A NATURAL MAGNET, THAT CAN BE USED IN SPELLWORK TO ATTRACT WHAT YOU DESIRE. ONCE YOU DECIDE TO USE LODESTONE IN A RITUAL YOU CANNOT REPURPOSE IT FOR ANOTHER RITUAL. TAKE CARE OF YOUR STONE BY NOT EXPOSING IT TO EXCESSIVE HEAT OR DROPPING IT. DOING SO CAN CAUSE IT TO LOSE ITS MAGNETIC ABILITIES. IF THAT HAPPENS BURY IT AND OBTAIN A NEW ONE.

Apple Magic

You can work with apples in many ways in spell work. Here are a few suggestions

- Cut an apple in half through the widest part. It will reveal a pentagram. Offer half of your apple to your altar and eat the rest to invoke your magic.
- Carve into an apple a word or symbol that represents your desires. Then eat it clockwise around until you reach the core.
- Collect 7 apple seeds and put them in a small envelope or mojo bag with cinnamon to attract love into your life.
- Take an apple and peel it from the top (where the stem is) to the bottom. As you are peeling the apple where at the point where it stops. Take the peel and throw it over your shoulder to reveal the first initial of your love's name.

PRIESTESS

ANOINTING OIL

TO BE USED IN RITUALS OF RITES OF PASSAGE, NEW BEGINNINGS, AND INITIATION

BLEND THE FOLLOWING ESSENTIAL OILS* IN A CARRIER OIL OF YOUR CHOICE. I PERSONALLY PREFER JOJOBA OIL FOR THIS ONE.

WHITE SAGE, ELEMI, COPAL, SANDALWOOD, MUSK AMBRETTE, PINK LOTUS BLOSSOM, AND CEDARWOOD

* WITH ESSENTIAL OILS A LITTLE GOES A LONG WAY. USE SPARINGLY AND WITH REVERANCE. DO NOT INGEST, FOR TOPICAL USE ONLY.

111
YOUR INTENTIONS ARE MANIFESTING

222
KEEP THE FAITH

333
ASCENDED MASTERS ARE ASSISTING YOU NOW

444
YOU ARE GUIDED + SUPPORTED BY YOUR ANGELS

555
BIG CHANGES ARE AHEAD. PACE YOURSELF.

666
YOU ARE INFINITE, DREAM BIGGER.

777
SPIRITUAL MYSTERY ESOTERIC WISDOM

888
WEALTH + PROSPERITY

999
END OR COMPLETION OF SOMETHING SIGNIFICANT

1111
MASTER MANIFESTOR SOUL'S ALIGNMENT WITH PURPOSE

000
NEW BEGINNINGS A FRESH START

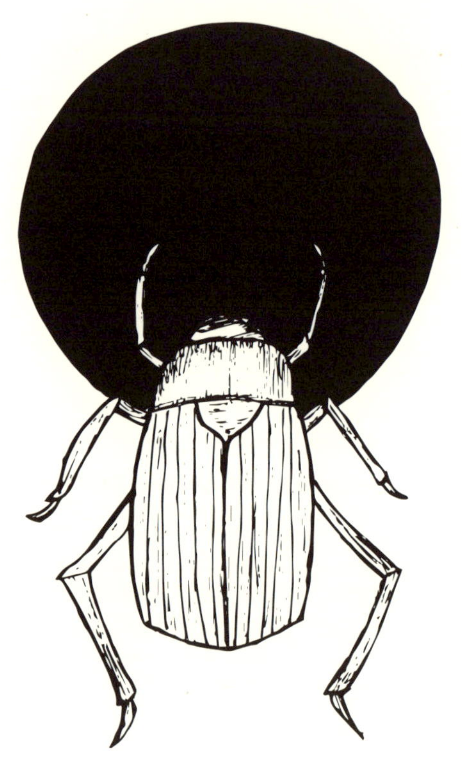

BLESSED BE THE LIVING
BLESSED BE THE DEAD
BLESSED BE THE SOUNDS
INSIDE MY HEAD

Haunted Hotel

-TRAVEL KIT-

I OFTEN GET WOKEN UP BY WAYWARD SPIRITS WHEN TRAVELING. I STARTED CARRYING THIS KIT TO ENSURE A RESTFUL NIGHT'S SLEEP.

— WHAT YOU NEED —

4 TUMBLED STONES → (Black TOURMaline, OBSIDIAN, selenite, AMETHYST)

1 TEALIGHT CANDLE

1 small bottle OF FLORIDA WATER

— WHAT TO DO —

WHEN YOU ARRIVE light the CANDLE AND GREET THE SPACE. THANK IT FOR TAKING CARE OF YOU FOR HOWEVER LONG YOU ARE THERE. PROMISE TO RESPECT IT AND CARE FOR IT AS IF IT WERE YOUR HOME. PLACE A STONE IN THE 4 OUTER MOST CORNERS OF THE ROOM. YOU CAN ANOINT YOURSELF, THE DOORWAYS, AND THE WINDOWS WITH THE FLORIDA WATER.

SCRYing

a form of divination by gazing into the SURface of objects

– Seeing Tools –

CRystal Ball, Obsidian MIRROR, water SURfaces, FIRE and Smoke

4 Psychic C's

Clairvoyance = Clear Seeing
LIKE WATCHING A MOVIE PLAY IN YOUR HEAD

Clairaudience = Clear Hearing
HEARING AUDITORY MESSAGES OUTSIDE THE PHYSICAL REALM, OFTEN DELIVERED VIA SPIRITS + GUIDES

Clairsentience = Clear Feeling
STRONG FEELINGS OR SHIFTS IN EMOTIONS AROUND ENERGY OR PEOPLE

Claircognizance = Clear Knowing
KNOWING THINGS ABOUT OTHERS WITHOUT PRIOR KNOWLEDGE

Once Upon A Time...

I STARTED READING TAROT NOT BECAUSE I WANTED BUT BECAUSE I HAD TO FIND REFUGE IN A WORLD THAT WOULD NOT SUPPORT MY STRANGE INESCAPABLE SENSITIVITY AFTER HAVING A NEAR DEATH EXPERIENCE. IT WAS THE 90'S IN PROVIDENCE, RHODE ISLAND. I HAD OVERDOSED AT A RAVE AND BASICALLY WOKE UP WITH ALL THE PSYCHIC LIGHTS TURNED ON. MAGIC, TAROT, AND THE OCCULT GAVE ME A PLACE TO NURSE MY BROKEN SPIRIT, AND SOMETHING TO LIVE FOR.

I HAD A DOUBLE LIFE CREATING ART AND MAGIC SEPARATELY FOR MANY YEARS. I DO MISS THE SECRET MEETINGS AND HIDING FOR HOURS WHILE RUMMAGING THROUGH BOOKS WITHIN DUSTY NEW ENGLAND WICCAN SHOPS. LISTENING TO CRONES AND WISDOM KEEPERS WITH OPEN EARS AND A CLOSED MOUTH. NOTHING IS THE SAME ANYMORE.

MY CRAFT IS AN OCCUPATION NOW, NO LONGER MY SECRET GARDEN. PROFESSIONAL HIGH PRIESTESS AT YOUR SERVICE. I LONG FOR A TIME WHEN IT WAS REVERED AND MYSTERIOUS. WHEN THE ORACLE WAS SHOWN RESPECT FOR THEIR OFFERINGS, INSTEAD OF A CAREFULLY CURATED FASHIONABLE LIST OF MUST HAVES OR BEING TOLD, "BE NICER YOU'LL BE MORE APPROACHABLE." WHAT IF I TOLD YOU THAT MY MAGIC NEVER CAME FROM BEING NICE? WHAT IF I TOLD YOU THAT THE TRUTH ABOVE ALL THINGS WAS THE ONLY THING THAT GOT ME HERE? WHAT IF I TOLD YOU IT'S NOT ALL PRETTY, FAIRES, GOLDEN LIGHT, AND ANGELS? WHAT IF I TOLD YOU THAT ANGELS (IF YOU EVER MET ONE) ARE ACTUALLY TERRIFYING AND BEAUTIFUL ALL AT ONCE, JUST LIKE YOUR SHADOW? WHAT IF, WHAT IF, WHAT IF, WE WERE TO ILLUMINATE THE REALITY WE ARE ALL HERE FOR. I'M READY. ARE YOU?

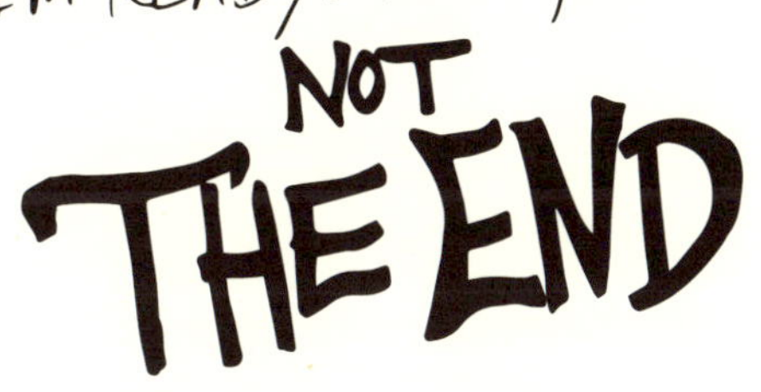

BORN from Light
RAISED BY DEATH
HER EMPATHY for
HER CAPTURES
CAUSED HER TO
grow HER
OWN SET
OF
HORNS.

NEVER BE SORRY FOR
EXCUSING POISON FROM
YOUR LIFE

STAY INSIDE THE SALT RING

A ring of salt around you or your spellwork will protect you and your rituals.

CLEAR ENERGY WITH SOUND

TO

PROTECT MY ENERGY

It's okay to change my mind
It's okay to cancel a commitment
It's okay to take a day off
It's okay to not answer a call
It's okay to not share myself
It's okay to do nothing
It's okay to be alone
It's okay to sleep in
It's okay to speak up
It's okay to move on
It's okay to let go
It's okay to change

POWERFUL ALLY FOR SCRYING, LUNAR MAGIC, PROTECTION, LUCID DREAMING, ASTRAL TRAVEL, AND VISION WORK.

BEST USED IN RITUAL BATHS, PSYCHIC TEAS,* DIVINATORY INCENSE, AND FLYING OINTMENTS

DREAM TEA RECIPE

IN A TEA BALL OR BAG, MIX A PINCH OF MUGWORT AND A PINCH OF DRIED LAVENDAR. STEEP IN HOT WATER FOR 3-5 MINUTES BEFORE BED

*USE WITH CAUTION WHEN INGESTING. OVER USE CAN CAUSE NIGHTMARES

ROAD OPENER

IDEALLY ROAD OPENER SPELLS ARE DONE DURING A WAXING MOON, WHEN YOU WANT TO DRAW IN NEW OPPORTUNITIES OR DURING A WANING MOON TO GET RID OF OBSTACLES ON YOUR PATH.

A SIMPLE SPELL FOR NEW OPPORTUNITIES

1 YELLOW CANDLE, ANOINTED WITH ESSENTIAL OILS OF ORANGE, LEMON BLOSSOM, AND CITRONELLA. CARVE A SIMPLE WORD OR SYMBOL FOR YOUR INTENTION. LIGHT YOUR CANDLE AND VISUALIZE A CLEAR OPEN ROAD TO YOUR GOAL. IF YOU SENSE OR SEE ANYONE OR ANYTHING BLOCKING YOUR WAY IMAGINE THEM GONE HARMLESSLY. THEN SAY ALOUD:

CLEAR THE PATH, CLEAR THE WAY
WITH HARM TO NONE SUCESS IS
MINE TO STAY

SKELETON KEYS

KEYS REPRESENT KNOWLEDGE AND ACCESS. POSESSING A KEY CAN GAIN YOU ACCESS AND SET BOUNDARIES. THEY CAN BE USED AS A TALISMAN OF PROTECTION, SAFE TRAVEL, AND AS A TOOL TO GET FROM ONE PLACE TO ANOTHER WITH EASE AND GRACE. CAN BE HUNG FROM DOORWAYS FOR PROTECTION. ALSO USED FOR OPENING ROADS AND CALLING SPIRITS.

HOW TO DISPOSE OF RITUAL REMNANTS

- IF YOU WANT TO KEEP SOMETHING CLOSE, BURY IT IN YOUR BACK YARD.
- IF YOU WANT TO ATTRACT SOMETHING, PUT IT UNDER YOUR FRONT DOOR STEP OR DOORMAT.
- IF YOU WANT TO DESTROY IT'S INFLUENCE, BURN IT.
- IF YOU WANT IT TO MOVE AWAY, THROW IT IN RUNNING WATER.
- IF YOU WANT TO EXPAND ITS INFLUENCE, THROW IT IN A CROSSROADS
- IF YOU WANT TO GROUND ITS INFLUENCE GRID IT IN A FIVE POINTED STAR PATTERN.
- IF YOU WANT TO HAVE THE ASSISTANCE OF SPIRITS, BURY IT IN A GRAVEYARD. (ASK THE SPIRITS IF IT'S OK FIRST)

AS ABOVE
SO BELOW

FIRE
AIR
WATER
EARTH
CONJOINED =
AS ABOVE
SO BELOW

When setting intentions try and imagine what you want your end result to feel like. Often times our spellwork will not manifest if we do not feel it is possible.

In conclusion I always like to add the following phrase to my spellwork to always invite in what's for the highest good.

"Please bring me this or something better than I can imagine, with harm to none, so mote it be!"

We belong to her

She does not belong to us

SALT BURN FOR PURIFICATION

(USE CAUTION WHEN WORKING WITH FIRE)

YOU WILL NEED:

- 1 FIRE SAFE POT OR DISPOSABLE ALUMINUM PAN
- 1 LARGER PAN TO SET THE SMALLER ONE IN
- TRIVET
- 1/4 EPSOM SALTS - CUP
- 3 TABLESPOONS OF RUBBING ALCOHOL (91%)
- LONG MATCH OR CANDLE TAPER LIGHTER

INSTRUCTIONS:

- PLACE SALT IN PILE IN PAN OR POT
- SET PAN IN LARGER PAN OR POT
- POUR ALCOHOL OVER SALT SATURATING IT
- SET ON TOP OF TRIVET - AWAY FROM ALL FLAMMABLE ITEMS, AND GIVE PLENTY OF SPACE AROUND THE POT SO IT DOES NOT IGNITE ANYTHING NEARBY
- KEEP EXTRA SALT NEARBY IN CASE YOU HAVE TO THROW SOME ON THE FLAMES TO EXTINQUISH IT
- LIGHT THE SALT + ALCOHOL, THEN CHANT

"I RELEASE ALL NEGATIVE ENERGIES, ENTITIES, AND PARASITIC BEINGS"

- STAND BACK AND LET IT BURN COMPLETELY
- ONCE FINISHED AND POT IS COOL TO TOUCH, FLUSH THE REMNANTS DOWN THE TOILET

MERRY MEET
MERRY PART
AND
MERRY MEET
AGAIN

NOTES

NOTES

NOTES

NOTES

MARCELLA KROLL IS A MULTIMEDIA ARTIST, RITUALIST, PSYCHIC MEDIUM, AND METAPHYSICAL TEACHER.

FIND OUT MORE ABOUT MARCELLA AT MARCELLAKROLL.COM

Kroll, Marcella

Second edition
Not a Cult

ISBN 978-1-945649-27-1

Illustrated by Marcella Kroll
Layout by Ian DeLucca
Cover design by Shaun Roberts

Printed in Canada